Full
of
Fall

April Pulley Sayre

Beach Lane Books • New York London Toronto Sydney New Delhi

September sun
is low in the sky.

So long, summer.
Green, goodbye!

One leaf.

Another leaf.

Colors surge.

Meet the trees!

Their shapes emerge.

Greetings, gold.

Oh—it's orange!

Red, be bold.

Leaves frame trunks,
light and dark.

Ripples.

Reflections.

Berries.

Bark.

Limbs and layers.

Leafy lanes.

Midribs.

Margins.

Sunlit veins.

But soon . . .

Trees are ready.

Twigs let go.

Leaves slip

and spin.

Wind sweeps—
leaves blow!

They drift and dry.

Their edges curl.

They float

and sink.

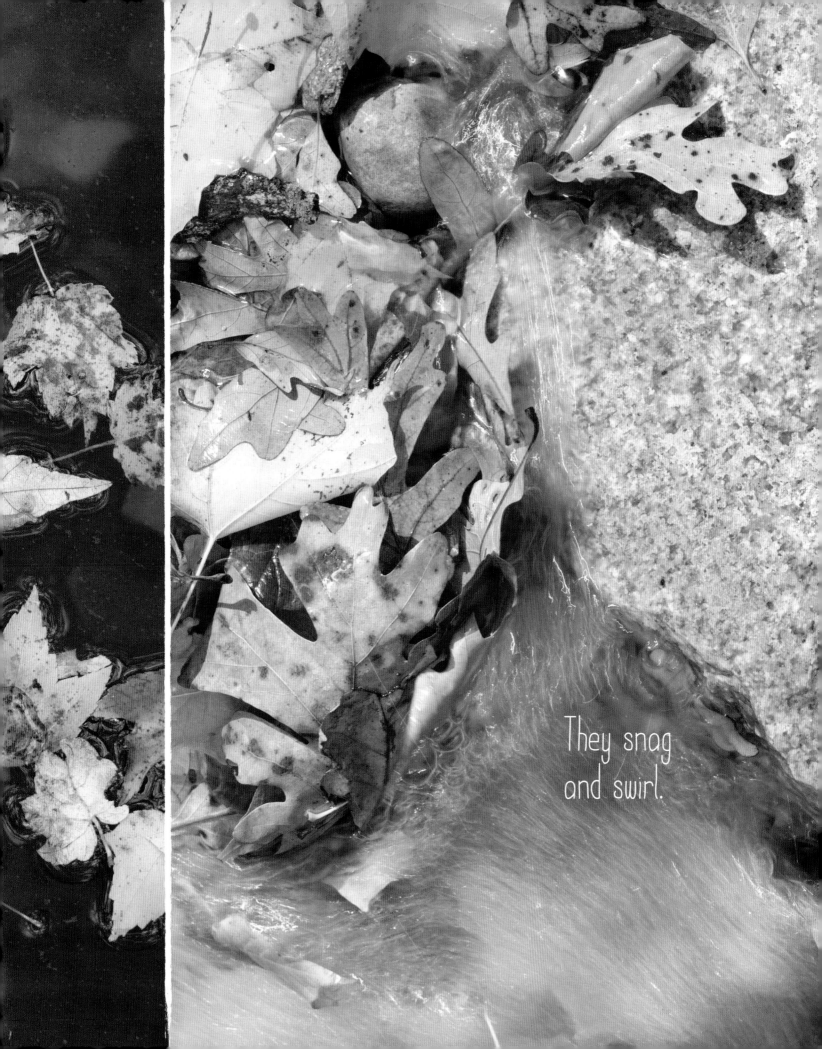

They snag
and swirl.

So many leaves!
The forest glows.

Leaves fade

and brown

and decompose.

Fall is ending.

Goodbye, leaf show.
Winter is coming. . . .

Oh,
hello, snow!

Look Closer: Leaves

As summer comes to a close, the sun traces a lower path in the sky. The air grows cooler. The days grow shorter and the nights grow longer. This change signals many plants to stop growing. Deciduous trees prepare to drop their leaves. The fall leaf show is beginning. . . .

Green, goodbye!

During spring and summer, a pigment called chlorophyll makes leaves green and captures light for photosynthesis. Using sunlight, water, and carbon dioxide from the air, photosynthesis produces sugars to power the plant and build roots, shoots, leaves, flowers, and seeds. But in late summer, growth slows. Leaves stop producing chlorophyll, and the green color fades.

Hello, yellow. Greetings, gold. Oh—it's orange!

The fall forest gets its colors from the very same varieties of pigments that make fruits and vegetables colorful. Carotenoid pigments—the kind of pigments that make carrots orange—are hidden in green leaves in spring and summer. When that green fades from leaves, the orange, gold, and yellow carotenoids show.

Red, be bold.

In fall, leaves also produce new pigments: red and purple anthocyanin. (Anthocyanin pigments are the ones that make raspberries red and grapes purple.) Scientists suspect anthocyanin may act as an autumn sunscreen, protecting the leaves until they drop. As leaves turn color they are still doing important work. They break apart chlorophyll, saving its important nutrients and sending them back into the tree for reuse.

Margins. Midribs. Sunlit veins.

Fall is a great time to appreciate a leaf's edges, called margins. Some leaves have a thickened central vein called a midrib. It helps support the leaf. Veins are bundles of xylem and phloem. Xylem carries water and nutrients to the leaf. Phloem carries sugars made by the leaf back to the rest of the plant.

Trees are ready. Twigs let go.

The leaves have done their job of powering the tree and cleaning up leftover chlorophyll. So the tree grows a separation layer between the leaf stem and the twig. This layer cuts off the supply of water and nutrients to the leaf. Some of the cells in the layer expand and break nearby, weaker cells. This helps disconnect the leaf from the tree. The leaf may fall on its own, or the wind and rain may help it break away.

Leaves fade and brown and decompose.

Scattered leaves aren't tree trash. They are more like gold, the wealth of the forest. Even after the chlorophyll cleanup, leaves still contain lots of nutrients. Leaves that fall into streams bring nutrients to the stream's insects and fish. On the forest floor, worms, beetles, snails, slugs, fungi, and bacteria break down the leaves into smaller pieces, and eventually into soil. One of the reasons the soil is so rich in the deciduous forests is because the leaves break down on the forest floor. Each autumn's leaf fall is one of the biggest transfers of energy in the natural world.

Oh, hello, snow!

By the time snow falls, deciduous trees have usually lost their leaves. But a few deciduous tree species, such as the American beech and some varieties of oak, are marcescent, meaning they wait until spring to drop their leaves. Other trees, called evergreens, don't shed all their leaves in one season. Evergreens lose leaves and grow new ones gradually throughout the year. Many evergreens have narrow leaves called needles that drop without most people noticing.

Fall around the world

Wherever fall occurs, its colors vary according to the dominant tree species. Mainland Eurasia has mostly yellow and gold trees. New England has vibrant yellow, orange, and red sugar maples. In Japan, red Japanese maples and golden ginkgo trees are the stars of the show. In South America, Chile and Argentina have forests that turn red, gold, and yellow. Meanwhile, cottonwood trees turn yellow along winding rivers in the western United States, and the Rocky Mountains are painted yellow by aspens.

Never the same show

The fall color show is full of variety. It isn't just made by trees but also by vines, shrubs, and other small plants that turn color. Yearly variations in the amount of sunlight, rainfall, and overall growing conditions create different leaf shades. If there's not enough rain in late summer, the tree leaves brown before they fall. Air temperatures that are low but still above freezing help produce the brightest reds. Each fall is unique. So get out and enjoy the show!

For
Lauren "Raindrops" Rille

THANK YOU, Andrea Welch, for creative
partnership. Thanks also to Barbara Murray
Ottewell, Potato Creek State Park, St. Patrick's
County Park, Fernwood, The Book Vine for
Children, Irene Garneau, Wintonbury Early
Childhood Magnet School, Beth Bye, Talcott
Mountain State Park, Karyn Lewis Bonfiglio,
and Megan Jessop. For scientific review, thank
you to Jeff Sayre and Professor John R. Seiler
of Virginia Tech.

Resources

Ehlert, Lois. *Leaf Man.* San Diego: Harcourt, 2005.

Salas, Laura Purdie. *A Leaf Can Be.* Minneapolis: Millbrook Press, 2012.

Sayre, April Pulley. *Squirrels Leap, Squirrels Sleep.* New York: Holt, 2016.

Sayre, April Pulley. *Trout Are Made of Trees.* Watertown, MA: Charlesbridge, 2008.

Schaefer, Lola, and Adam Schaefer. *Because of an Acorn.* San Francisco: Chronicle Books, 2016.

BEACH LANE BOOKS An imprint of Simon & Schuster Children's Publishing Division • 1230 Avenue of the Americas, New York, New York 10020 • Copyright ©
2017 by April Pulley Sayre • All rights reserved, including the right of reproduction in whole or in part in any form. • BEACH LANE BOOKS is a trademark of Simon & Schuster,
Inc. • For information about special discounts for bulk purchases, please contact Simon & Schuster Special Sales at 1-866-506-1949 or business@simonandschuster.com.
• The Simon & Schuster Speakers Bureau can bring authors to your live event. For more information or to book an event, contact the Simon & Schuster Speakers Bureau at
1-866-248-3049 or visit our website at www.simonspeakers.com. • Book design by Lauren Rille • The text for this book is set in Quickrest and Bodoni. • Manufactured in
China • 0617 SCP • First Edition • 10 9 8 7 6 5 4 3 2 1 • Library of Congress Cataloging-in-Publication Data • Names: Sayre, April Pulley, author. • Title: Full of
fall / April Pulley Sayre. • Description: First edition. | New York :: Beach Lane Books, An imprint of Simon & Schuster Children's Publishing Division [2017] | Audience: Age
4–8. | Audience: K to grade 3. | Includes bibliographical references and index. • Identifiers: LCCN 2016053599 | ISBN 9781481479844 | ISBN 9781481479851 (eBook) •
Subjects: LCSH: Autumn—Juvenile literature. | Seasons—Juvenile literature. • Classification: LCC QB637.7.S285 2017 | DDC 508.2—dc23 LC record available at https://
lccn.loc.gov/2016053599